THE MUSE OF THE VIOLETS

POEMS BY

RENEE VIVIEN

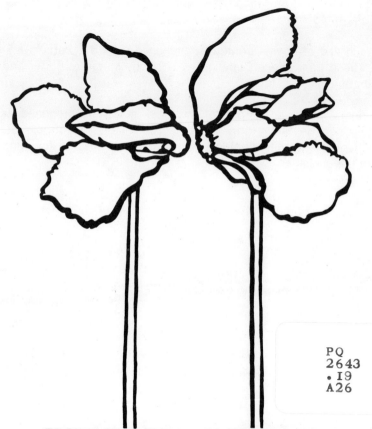

TRANSLATED FROM THE FRENCH BY
MARGARET PORTER & CATHARINE KROGER

THE NAIAD PRESS INC.
1977

French text, Introduction, in Mercure de France, I-XII-1953, at page 633. This translation Copyright © 1977 by The Naiad Press, Incorporated.

French text of poems printed by Alphonse Lemerre, Paris, 1923-24. These translations Copyright © 1977 by Margaret Porter and Catharine Kroger.

Printed in the United States of America
First Edition

Cover illustration:
Designed and executed by Tee A. Corinne

ISBN:0-930044-07-X
Library of Congress Catalog Card Number 77-77988

PUBLISHER'S NOTE

This is the first time that any of the poetry of Renée Vivien (pseudonym of the Anglo-American lesbian, Pauline Tarn, 1877-1909) has appeared in English in book form. In their French originals, her poems have always been recognized by critics as some of the finest examples of the classical French mode. Our translators here present selections in two distinct styles. Margaret Porter has successfully attempted to project in English the meter and rhyme of the French, while capturing its emotional quality. Catharine Kroger has used a freer style to convey in English the brilliant imagery of the French.

The Introduction, which consists of an excerpt from a memoir by a contemporary of Renée Vivien, gives a vivid glimpse of the Muse of the Violets. The translation by Jeannette H. Foster captures the sympathetic quality of Mme. Faure-Favier's reminiscence.

Renée Vivien

THE MUSE OF THE VIOLETS*

By

Louise Faure-Favier

(Translated from the French by Jeannette H. Foster)

In 1906 the poet Renée Vivien, at that time already famous for her volumes of poems, ETUDES ET PRELUDES and CENDRES ET POUSSIERES, got the idea of writing in prose for the weekly journals. That was how it came about that one October morning I was sent to deliver to her the third number of THE CRITIC, which contained her first article, "Jesus Christ and the Reporter."

I quickly covered the short distance from the rue Belles-Feuilles to the Avenue Bois de Boulogne. Here she who was called the muse of the violets lived in a luxurious first-floor apartment which opened on a Japanese garden bordering the Avenue. I had thought that afterwards I would stroll down the long stretch of the Bois to enjoy the autumn day. But Renée Vivien's maid said that Mademoiselle wished to thank me.

---

*Published in the Mercure de France, I-XII-53, at page 633. The present text is an excerpt from the article.

7

Thus I saw by daylight the drawingroon that I had never before entered except for the magnificent evening affairs to which I had gone with my husband. Now the heavy black velvet drapes no longer covered the high windows. I could admire the splendid furniture brought from the Far East, the iridescent glassware from Ceylon and Daum and all the buddhas before which incense burners gave off a mixture of perfumes. And the flowers! Too much incense and too many flowers! I would have loved to open one of those stained glass windows.

Why stained glass? Isn't light beloved of poets? I should have liked to let in that morning light, if only to see better the portrait of Renée Vivien which hung in the shadows.

The portrait, painted by Lévy-Dhurmer, showed her against a background of ultramarine blue. This set off well the coronet of blonde hair that revealed her youthful forehead. The head was small, as in a Tanagra figurine, the features delicate. But I could not find there the changing expression of those brown eyes flecked with gold that I remembered, nor the lovely smile of those finely cut lips that showed white and even teeth. Nor had the artist caught the expressiveness of her eyelids--"cool lids of the eyes of Beatrice."

Nevertheless, I knew that this portrait, which only her close friends in Paris had seen, was as much appreciated in England as her poetic talent. Booksellers in London had reproductions made which sold for very high prices. But Renée Vivien, when she learned of this,

8

hastened to forbid their sale.

After the portrait I next examined a statuette before which a watchlight burned night and day, it was said. And it was also whispered that this was an image of Sappho brought by Renée Vivien from the Isle of Lesbos. But what won't people say? They even said that this Sappho was honored each morning with ritual offerings of incense and flowers.

This cult of paganism bothered me. It made me want to laugh and at the same time to get out of there.

*   *   *

"No, it isn't Sappho," said Renée Vivien, who had come in with her light step, wearing an empress's kimono and carrying a sheaf of roses in her arms, which she offered me by way of greeting.

Mutual thanks followed. Then:

"That's only a Vestal I bought in Athens because she looks like a friend I've lost, a dead friend I can't forget. When I am desperately sad I pray to her, as pagans pray to their idols and Christians to their saints."

"Oh!" I gasped, really shocked. But at her expression of deep melancholy I hastened to add:

"Forgive me, mademoiselle. I am only a little provincial who is not yet wholly accustomed to Parisian life. I am just discovering--and am frightened by--the literary world. Still, please believe that I admire your poetic gifts very much. I know by heart your beautiful poem 'The Trees.'"

Renée Vivien smiled, because that was one of the few

poems among her works that was not of lesbian inspiration. She offered me her hand, disarmed by such frankness. She even declared that I pleased her because I was so healthy and sane and uncomplicated, a really wise Frenchwoman who would never become an "aesthete" after the fashion of women of la belle epoque.

And I, emboldened by her sincerity, told her that I felt a deep sympathy for her; a tenderness inspired by her obvious fragility, her extreme thinness, her pallor. She seemed hardly a creature of this world; and I would have liked to see her stronger, a little more real. I actually said this to her.

She answered with a weary gesture:

"I was born under an unlucky star. I love France and I am not French. I am English and I can't like England. My father was Scotch, my mother was born in Honolulu. My father, William* Tarn, died at the age of forty in 1890. My real name is Pauline Tarn. I changed it to Renée Vivien."

"But the name Pauline is lovely," I told her. "It was the name of Mme. de Sevigné's granddaughter. And Tarn is the name of a French province."

"That's quite true. I'm not logical. I'm infected with the romantic fever. It began in my teens when I read Baudelaire in secret, in a country boarding school in England from which I slipped away by climbing over the wall. I was fifteen, the same age as Juliet--a Juliet for

_____

*Translator's note: Most reference books give his name as John.

10

whom Romeo had no attraction."

"Why?"

She gave me this strange answer: "Men smell of leather."

"Leather! What kind of leather?"

"The leather of huntsmen, furniture movers, porters."

"But you know plenty of cultivated men, and they admire you. Didn't you learn your Greek from the great classicist Charles Brun, who was so enthusiastic about his pupil that at the end of two years he said, 'Mademoiselle, I have nothing more to teach you. You know Greek better than I do.'"

"He was too lenient, Charles Brun," she answered. "He was so charming that I always write to him as 'My dear Charlotte!'"

"And Eugene Ledrain who coached you in Latin, and said of you, 'What intelligence, what learning, how much poetry in that handsome little head!'"

"Well, I can't write 'My dear Eugenie' to him, because the stern Mme. Ledrain opens all his letters."

"...Just once in my life a man tried to embrace me. It was horrible! He had big boots, a heavy belt, huge gloves. Faugh! Oh, let's not talk about men."

"All right, let's talk of your travels."

I envied Renée Vivien for having, though so young, travelled over so much of the world. She knew China, then still so mysterious. She knew America, then so far away. She had crossed the Pacific, at least as far as the Sandwich Islands. She had spent several winters in Egypt!

11

All the European capitals were well-known to her. Greece had so captivated her that she now owned a small house at Mytilene. From Constantinople, where she had lived in a palace above the Bosphorus, she had gone to Syria! She gave a poet's description of the ruins at Balbec and the gardens of Damascus... Happy Renée Vivien, to know all these charmed places! She was a marvel to me, a little French girl who had not even crossed the Swiss frontier and who only dreamed of such distant travels. But for her, travel meant only escape from a life of disillusion, while for me it would have held all the excitement of discovery.

I listened to that voice, so melancholy, saying:

"Yes, I've seen all that, and I have come back wanting to see more, to see something different--to look till I become blind. To see everything on earth--to see even further, into the beyond!"

It was then that I dared suggest that she might regain inspiration by putting these memories of a vagabond Muse into poems that would be so beautiful!

"Perhaps, some day, later," she answered.

And that became LE VENT DES VAISSEAUX, the unfinished volume that appeared after her death.

*   *   *

But on that October morning there was no thought of death. We parted gaily with her promise to attend the next Sunday reception of The Political and Literary Critic.

Renée Vivien did not need to be begged to accept. She

who swore that she disliked going out came quite simply, dressed in black. Her simplicity, her diffidence astonished everyone. Instead of a Baudelarian halo, our Muse of the Violets wore only her coronet of ash blonde tresses and the chignon of a quiet and well-bred English miss.

Looking at that pale face, that lack of curves, Tristan Bernard said a cruel thing: "She makes me doubt my own sex."

And the women? What did they think?

It is said that women have a different concept of feminine beauty from men. They are sensitive to regularity and delicacy of features. "Prettiness" pleases them. Extreme thinness is not distasteful. Beautiful eyes, of course. A smallish curving mouth. And above all, a flawless complexion. Hair heavy and waving--ah, yes, luxurious hair is important. Elegance, too, and even more, distinction. A graceful walk is acceptable, but women frown on too much development of the hips or those swaying movements that hold the attention of men. We need not mention the legs, always completely hidden by long skirts. One hardly glimpsed a foot. But Renée Vivien's feet were small and high-arched. All this is why, that afternoon, all the women found Renée Vivien ravishing.

As to Renée herself, indifferent to the contradictory effects she produced, she left as unobtrusively as she had come.

She reappeared one evening--and this time she was very elegantly and formally dressed--to hear Georgette Leblanc

read from PELLÉAS ET MÉLISANDE and sing the famous aria
from the second act.

Wearing a long necklace of lalique with her white
gown, a touch of rouge on her cheeks, Renee Vivien quite
seduced all the young poets who surrounded her. Emile
Verhaeren complimented her gravely. Present that night
were Maurice Maeterlinck, André Foulon de Vaux, Firmin
Roz, Alexandre Arnoux, Leo Larguier, René Fauchois, Hugues
Lapaire, Andre Delacour, Adolphe Lacuzon, Maurice Magre--
all happy and proud to meet this poet whom they admired,
as connoisseurs, for the perfection of classical form in
her verse, its harmonious rhythm, the purity of her
French. The impulsive Lucien Rolmer, instead of listening
to the program, composed a sonnet in honor of the Muse of
the Violets, of which she had to listen to every word. As
to the southerner Joachim Gasquiet, he dropped on one knee
to declare himself "infinitely honored to kiss the hand
which writes such beautiful verse." To all these
compliments she responded graciously. Feeling closely
attuned to all poets, she had read their works and knew
how to discuss them. Her praise of LA MAISON DU POETE/THE
POET'S HOUSE/ went straight to the heart of Leo Larguier,
who never forgot it or her.

She left each of them with an enchanted memory.

This time she did not "take English leave." She let
someone see her all the way to her carriage.

*   *   *

Some time later I received from her one of those
elegant letters written on vellum bordered with garlands

14

of violets and sealed with gold wax:

"I was wrong to say that no one ever remembers anything heard at a lecture. Forget those foolish words! I have caught the lecture fever, in my turn. I am going to give one, at home, Sunday at the hour of Vespers. There will be an enormous audience of three! Will you make a fourth? We will lunch beforehand, at one o'clock."

It was an original lecture! It took place in the garden of Japanese arbors into which the French windows of the salon opened, their curve-topped halves shaped like wings. All the shrubbery was in bloom and every flower was heavily scented. The thick ivy on the wrought iron grille separated us from the Avenue and the rest of the world. We, the four listeners, sat on the grass of the smooth lawn and Renée Vivien, leaning back against a genista, rose above us by the height of a footstool.

It was a charming lecture! Miss Natalie Barney, Miss Patricia, do you remember it? The speaker hadn't even chosen her subject. She asked us to suggest something from Ibsen for her to discuss. We chose BRAND and THE QUEST OF THE ABSOLUTE.

"There's a proper subject for a lecture at the Odeon by a bald-headed scholar!" she said with a laugh.

Still, for an hour she improvised on these themes and held us all spellbound under the charm of her easy and musical speech. And a Renée Vivien was revealed to us who was something of a mystic, very different from that pagan poet I so disapproved of for that verse:

"Oh, Christ so feared in the hour of our passing,

15

I have never known Thee, I do not know Thee now..."

But in these days people didn't broach religious subjects in a drawingroom as they do today, when anyone will argue theology between two cocktails. If the spectacular conversion of the jovial Huysmans still amused the skeptics, on the other hand it displeased those who modestly concealed their faith in the secret chambers of their hearts.

Nevertheless, I was not much surprised when, shortly afterward, Renée Vivien wrote that beautiful book, A L'HEURE DES MAINS JOINTES, and I read there:

"I believe in God and I love him. Formerly I believed in him and hated him. Today I love him and accept everything from him, because he made my soul which, after all, is me; and my body, although I do not despise my body either, for it resembles my soul."

It was at Bayreuth, it seems, while listening to PARSIFAL, that under the influence of the music she became conscious for the first time, though still very vaguely, of the voice of God...

In the meantime she remained pretty much a pagan and she was wholly given over to pleasure. She continued to live in great luxury, but it was not a life without worries. For we learned, much later, that she had just lost all hope of a large fortune which she went to Hawaii to see about, accompanied by her mother. They returned together, disappointed--the money was lost, though for a year afterward they continued to receive small sums.

But in the spring of 1908 she still lived in hope and

16

found life good. And what opportunities she had for diversion, she who loved the theatre and all the arts! Even so, this belle epoque was not altogether enchanting to her.

"What a disgrace to live at the beginning of the 20th century," she said to us that afternoon, from the eminence of her footstool. "One is always influenced by one's own time. And ours is that of Sarah Bernhardt and Rostand. Things will be much better in another ten years. You will see a new art born, new and beautiful. You will see that, but I shall not. I shall be dead. But--" she finished, laughing, "Sarah Bernhardt will live forever, and go on playing L'AIGLON forever!"

At that moment, however, her critical sense deceived her. She was forgetting that she, like all her contemporaries, had fallen under the spell of the great tragic actress. Had it not pleased her also to appear as a "queen of poseurs" when, visiting the Cathedral at Chartres, she swathed herself from head to foot--even her face--in thin veils the color of ashes, after the fashion of a priestess of antiquity? Thus costumed, she stood before the Cathedral entrance explaining the significance of the ancient stones with a "scholar's accuracy and the words of a poet," to the amazement and delight of visitors.

"Queen of poseurs" she was once again on the day when, invited to the wedding of a relative, she was seen advancing in the bridal procession, a figure out of fairy land, crowned with lilies, trailing long scarves of

glimmering white silk, in her arms a sheaf of lilies so
immense it seemed to clothe her entirely.

*   *   *

The end of the year 1908 was ill-starred for Renée
Vivien. She made apologies for ceasing to hold her
receptions. She left for a long trip around the world. Or
at least that is what she wrote us from Cherbourg.
Actually she went no farther than London, where in a
moment of despondency she attempted to kill herself. She
drank laudanum, and stretched herself on one of those
divans "deep as a tomb" which were affected by the
Baudelarian cult even in puritanic England. With a bouquet
of violets over her heart, she hoped to go to sleep
forever.

Poor Muse of the Violets, ruinously in debt, so
learned, so gifted, but incapable of facing life's common
wounds! She was saved by the devotion of her faithful
maid, and so secretly that her friends knew nothing of the
incident. In Paris the complete silence with regard to her
was not surprising. We imagined her voyaging over the
seven seas and we now referred to her only as the Far-Away
Poetess.

She finally recovered and even returned to Paris but
she was shattered, unsteady on her feet, afflicted with
all manner of ills. One day as I was riding up the
Champs-Elysées in a taxi I spied her in a cab, sunk low in
the seat, her eyes closed, the mere shadow of herself. The
next day I called at her home to learn her latest news. I
ran head on into a message I knew to be a lie:

18

"Mademoiselle has been in Nice for a month and will not be back until April."

I saw her once more, one day in the summer of 1909. She was walking feebly, supported on one side by a cane, on the other by the arm of her maid. It was only because of the latter that I knew her--she herself was unrecognizable. It was an old woman passing. And she was only thirty-one! How long ago it seemed, the time when, imagining the decline of old age, she wrote these prophetic lines:

"Your step will forget the rhythm of waves.

Your flesh empty of desire, your stiffening limbs

Will no longer tremble with profound ardor.

Love, disenchanted, will no longer recognize you."

She died on November 10, 1909, in Paris, on her return from England, when the pleurisy she contracted while there ended by taking its toll of a system weakened by deliberate fasting.

We learned later that she had abandoned Protestantism before her death; that she died quite simply, murmuring the name of that "Lorely" she had loved so dearly. She was heard to declare also: "I do not regret having written any verse that was beautiful." Was she remembering then her own poignantly melancholy lines:

"Yes, you will go to join your brothers, the poets

And they will welcome you into their ordered ranks

With their soundless voices and their mute lips."

Her death was almost unnoticed, with only a few brief obituaries in the papers. The literary world was at the moment all agog over the approaching performances of CHANTICLEER, and the question as to whether Mme. Simone, playing the pheasant, would or would not lay an egg on stage.

Still, the real poets of 1910 did not see her go without grief. There were a good many of us who mourned the passing of a talent which approached genius in its moments of loveliest flowering. None of us was unaware that some loving hands kept her grave blossoming constantly with her favorite violets. Even today some faithful friend keeps up the little chapel where she sleeps in Passy cemetery.

POEMS

By

Renée Vivien

Translated by

Margaret Porter

To You for whom She wrote,
so that more of you
will remember her.

-Margaret A. Porter

CHANSON

The pomp of jewels, the vanity of curled tresses
Mix the polish of art with your perverse charm.
Even the gardenias which winter cannot harm
Die in your hands of your impure caresses.

Your delicately delineated mouth expresses
The artifice, the inflections of poetry.
Your breasts blossom in pale luxury
Under the cleverly half-open folds of your dresses.

The reflection of sapphires darkens in the somber night
Of your eyes. Your undulous body that troubles my sight
Makes a gleaming furrow of gold in the middle of the
   night.

When you pass, holding a subtle smile for me,
Blonde pastel surcharged with gems and perfumery,
I dream of the splendor of your body naked and free.

CHANSON

Your voice is a knowing poem to cajole
And charm me till all reason perishes.
I love you, oh dearest despair of my soul,
As a sorrow that one nurtures and cherishes.

Slim, tall, graceful, white,
Your return from the distant days of before,
My remote friend, oh flower of light,
Pale as the lilies that I adore.

A memory dulls and fades, I am told.
But how forget? I can never,
That your voice made itself soft to enfold
Me, to tell me you would love me forever.

*

*   *

Your form is a gleam that leaves me clutching emptiness.
Your smile is the moving instant that one can never clasp.
You flee when my avid lips implore you, seek you, press
Upon you, escaping my grasp.

More cold than visionary hope, your cruel caress
Dies like a pale reflection, passes like a faint perfume.
Oh, the eternal hunger, the eternal thirst for your
loveliness,
And the eternal regret, the doom.

You touch without embracing--Chimera one can see
That one strives for, reaches for and, over and over,
forever misses.
Nothing is worth this torment, not the bitter ecstasy,
Even, of your rare kisses.

SUNRISE ON THE SEA

> ...as for my sobbing: let the stormy
> winds carry it away for all suffering!
> —Sappho

Momentary pain, I disdain you at last.
I have lifted up my head. I have ceased to weep.
My soul is delivered, and your negligible ghost
No longer comes to graze it on nights of no sleep.

At the dawn which violates I smile today.
Without flower fragrance, oh wind of the enormous sea
Whose sharp odor of salt revives the force in me,
Oh wind of the wide sea, carry sorrows away.

Forever! Sweep sorrow into distance with a mighty blow
Of your wing, so that happiness will flare forth,
 triumphal,
In our hearts wherein divine pride springs anew,
Hearts turned toward the sun, song, and the ideal!

CHANSON

The bat in bizarre, twisting flight,
Beating his bruised and anguished wings,
Turns, returns, circles, flings
Himself crazily toward the blinding light.

Just for a moment did you not hear
How, drunk with futile misery,
My lost soul hurled itself frantically
Toward your lips so far away, so dear?

LUCIDITY

You fill your leisure with the delicate art of vice,
You know how to awaken the warmth of desire in ice.
Every movement of your supple body is a subtle caress;
The odor of the bed mingles with the perfumes of your
   dress.
The too-sweet blandness of honey is like your blond charm,
You love only the artificial, what does harm,
The music of elegant words and murmurings.
Your kisses graze the lips like transient wings.
Your eyes are winters starred with icy isles.
Lamentings follow your steps in dejected files.
Your word is a shadow, your gesture a pale reflection.
Your body has softened from kisses without affection,
Your soul has become withered, your body has been abused.
Languorous, lewd, your cunning touch you have used
Till it does not know the loyal beauty of the embrace.
You say the artful speeches one would hear, to one's face;
Beneath feigned sweetness a watchful reptile lies.
Dark as a sea without reflecting skies,
The tombs are less impure than your bed. But the worst,
Oh Woman! Only your mouth will quench my thirst!

Études et Préludes

SONNET

Oh form that hands will never know how to retain!
Elusive as a brief rainbow after rain,
Your smile, disappearing, leaves more empty, more drear,
The heart that mourns after a too-sweet souvenir.

How rejuvenate your caprice, tired, overdrawn,
So that it will flourish again with the freshness of dawn?
What words murmur, what rare lily make flower
To enchant away the ennui of leisure and the hour?

With what kisses charm the languor in which your soul
  sleeps
Until, exasperated of ecstasy,
Your avid, suppliant being swoons and weeps?

With what graceful rhythm of love, with what fervent poem
Honor her tempting beauty worthily
Who wears Desire on her forehead like a diadem?

CHANSON

I do not anymore wish to see
The world except through the veil
Of your hair, so blonde, so pale,
For my soul is weary of my destiny.

On my forehead that deliriums importune,
Over my sleepless eyes that stare,
Spread out the soft strands of hair
That seem to me gleaming rays of the moon.

Since the bitter past weeps alone,
Make of that gentle tissue of cloud
For spent hopes, lost dreams, a shroud,
And for joys I have ever-so-briefly known.

MODERN NAIAD

The pace of the times swirls in the cut of your dress.
Your body seems a net of wires, twisted by stress.
You attract and repel me like the unseen abyss
Hidden by the churning waves. Your hands dismiss
As they beckon. Your hair drips in tangled strands
Like seaweed. Your voice grates like the rasp of sands
And pebbles pulled by the suck of water. Your vague smile
Flickers like the glint of sun on a foam-washed pile.
Your forehead recalls the surface glass of the sea.
And your eyes cast me the lure of mediocrity.

A CRY

Through their half-closed lids your amorous blue eyes
Harbor vague betrayals, pleasant lies.
The violent, deceitful breath of these roses keeps
Me drunk like a wine in which slow poison sleeps.

Towards the evening hour when the fireflies madly dance
Our desire of the moment burns, reflects in your glance.
You repeat, in vain, your words of flattery...
I hate you and yet I love you abominably.

CHANSON

Opulent as the sunset, your mass
    Of rose-blonde hair.
And oh, Beloved, when you pass
    What trembling of the air!

Your silence is the darkness yet illumed
    After a song closes.
My giddy soul is all perfumed
    Of your flesh and white roses.

When you lift your lids your pale eyes
    Of a subtle, penetrating blue
Reflect the large lights of wide skies.
    "April!" the flowers say of you.

SLEEP

Your sleep terrifies me. It is as cold and profound
As eternal sleep. You make no smallest sound.
I am afraid of your closed eyes, of the calm of your face.
I watch for a movement of the long lashes to erase
The night behind your lids. Only stillness all around.

Foretasting mortal sorrow, final doom,
I do not know that your breath has not fled like the
    breath
Of the flowers, without agony or rattle of death,
Into distant night where dawn succumbs in the gloom
And that this bed of love is not already the tomb.

VELLEITY

Loosen your feverish arms, oh my mistress, dismiss
Me. Set me free from the yoke of your bitter kiss.
Far from your lascivious, oppressive scent,
Far from the languors of the bed where our hours are
  spent,

On the breath of the wind I shall breathe the sharp salt
  air,
The acrid tang of the algae; till clean and bare,
I shall go towards the wild profundity of the sea,
Pale from solitude, drunk with chastity.

EPITAPH

Softly you drifted from sleep into death,
From night to the tomb, from dream to silence,
As the sob of a chord fades on the breath
Of a summer evening that dies of somnolence.
Where colors confuse in the twilight deepening,
Where the world pales under the ashes of dream,
To the backward flow of the sap you seem
To listen and to April which makes the flowers sing.
With mute caresses, in its velvet keep
Earth holds you; on your forehead violets weep.

PROLONG THE NIGHT

> ...If it was permitted to Sappho
> to ask in her prayers "that the night
> be doubled for her," why should I not
> dare, on my turn, implore a similar
> favor...
>
> > -Libanios.

Prolong the night, Goddess who set us aflame!
Hold back from us the golden-sandalled dawn!
Already on the sea the first faint gleam
     Of day is coming on.

Sleeping under your veils, protect us yet,
Having forgotten the cruelty day may give!
The wine of darkness, wine of the stars let
     Overwhelm us with love!

Since no one knows what dawn will come,
Bearing the dismal future with its sorrows
In its hands, we tremble at full day, our dream
     Fears all tomorrows.

Oh! keeping our hands on our still-closed eyes,
Let us vainly recall the joys that take flight!
Goddess who delights in the ruin of the rose,
     Prolong the night!

THE TOUCH

The trees have kept some lingering sun in their branches.
Veiled like a woman, evoking another time,
The twilight passes, weeping. My fingers climb,
Trembling, provocative, the line of your haunches.

My ingenious fingers wait when they have found
The petal flesh beneath the robe they part.
How curious, complex, the touch, this subtle art--
As the dream of fragrance, the miracle of sound.

I follow slowly the graceful contours of your hips,
The curves of your shoulders, your neck, your unappeased
    breasts.
In your white voluptuousness my desire rests,
Swooning, refusing itself the kisses of your lips.

DEPARTURE

I have seen the flames of burning despair die out of me.
My mouth will cease to ravage your mouth with fierce
    caress.
I shall no longer know the stark and lonely distress
Of nights of savage desire and fevered sleeplessness,

For I am recalled tonight by death and the sea...

Darkness comes to drown your hair of asphodele light.
The bats beat, bruising their wings, against my door.
Blue and long the shadows weep across my floor.
I have stilled my heart where anguish was my inquisitor,

For the sea and death, at last, restore me tonight...

THE ROCKET

Dizzily I rocketed toward the stars through the night...
Compared to my pride, the triumph of the gods grew pale,
And my wildly joyous ascending nuptial flight
Tore away the shadows of summer like a fragile veil...

In a fleeing hymeneal kiss, I was the lover
Of the night, her hair tangled with violets.
I saw the white tobacco flowers uncover
Their caskets where sleep the memories one forgets.

And I saw, high and still higher, the divine Pleiades...
I attained Eternal Silence by my long escalade...
Then I broke like a false rainbow that the sun succeeds,
Casting feeble splinters of gold and onyx and jade...

I was the dream destroyed and the lightning spent...
I had known the ardor and the effort of the upward fight,
The victory and the monstrous fright of descent,
I was the fallen star which drowns in the night.

REMEMBRANCE

From your lips, Atthis, I have drunk burning wine in the
    night.
    The tenacity of embraces that clasp and enclose,
The clever complicity of the lowered light,
    The languors of the lily, the blushes of the rose!

In your robe, fluid, imprecise as the waves of the sea,
    You are like an algae. Your perfume, bitter, rare,
Evokes wisely your remembered nudity
    Where flowed your blonde Nereid hair.

TO THE UNKNOWN DIVINITY

Close to you I breathe silence and the witchery
Of nights where sorrow pleases itself to stay,
You whom one never sees wipe a tear away,
But the weeping of your great soul sometimes comes to me.

The mirror reflects your modest attitudes,
You shun pomp, make-up, artificiality.
Your lips have kept the fold of long solitudes
And the accent of good fortune come too late to be.

The scene of your lamentation is a tranquil room
Where the distant sound of waters dies languidly.
The breaths of the sea have scarcely lifted the gloom
Of perpetual evening in the shade of the drapery.

Toward you rises the pure aspiration of my soul.
My anguish does not seek to quench itself at all.
Unknown, you exist only in dream. This
Is why I adore you above and beyond the kiss.

*

*   *

I loved you, Atthis, long ago.

The evening makes flower again faded delights,
The reflection of your eyes, the tone of your voice,
   through my tears...
I loved you, Atthis, other days and nights,
      The length of the distant years.

*

*   *

...you forget me...

The troubled water reflects, like a vain looking-glass,
My pallid eyelids, my eyes too dull for gleams.
I listen to your laugh and your voice in the evening
   as you pass...
      Atthis, you have forgotten our dreams.

You have never known, of love, the warm lethargy,
The terror of the kiss, nor known the pride of hate;
You have wanted only the roses of a day from me,
      Uncertain love for whom I wait.

*

*   *

Atthis, my thought is detestable to
you, and you flee toward Andromeda.

You despise my thought, Atthis, and my image.
This other kiss, which persuades you from me,
Inflames you. Breathless and savage,
      Toward Andromeda you flee.

*

    *   *

For Andromeda, she has a beautiful
recompense.

For Andromeda: the lightning of your kiss, your unrests,
Your veils of a virgin, Atthis, to her you run
With your languors of a lover, the slow sigh of your
   unappeased breasts,
       Oh faithless one!

For Andromeda: the gold-brown evenings, the songs,
The shadow of your lashes on your pupils through the
   magic hours,
The nights of Lesbos where exalts a fragrance that belongs
      to eternal flowers.

For me: favored, fitful sleep under the skies
Where die the Pleiades; and the grave cadences,
The winter of your voice, the cold rhyme of your eyes,
      Your pale silences.

*

*   *

The stars around the beautiful moon
veil their clear faces when, in her
full, she illumines the earth with
gleams of silver.

All is white where the moon pours her shower.
At her feet groans the tormented sea.
Serene, she sees solitude flower
        In the night, and chastity.

Before divine Selene the stars
Have veiled their shining faces, and the white,
Snowing from the candid sky, scars
        The earth with silver light.

*

*   *

The dawn came to me in golden
sandals.

My eyes have seen dawn fleeing in sandals of gold:
On the taciturn mountain-top her swift feet gleam,
On treetops of the forest whose sleeping depths yet enfold
        The nocturnal dream.

*

*   *

Sleep on the breast of your
gentle mistress.

Sleep between the breasts of the conquered love. Rest,
Oh virgin in whose glance a brash adolescent gleams,
And let nuptial Hesperus lead you in your passionate quest
        Toward happy dreams.

*

*   *

Come, Goddess of Cyprus, and
pour delicately into the golden
cups the nectar mixed with joys.

Daughter of Kuprôs, whose lightning glance destroys,
Delicately with your graceful hands tip up
And pour the nectar mixed of bitterness and joys
        Into each golden cup.

*

*   *

...as to my sob: and that
the stormy winds carry it away
for sufferings.

Let the evening wind carry away my sob
Towards the prostrate cities and plains of vague
    tomorrows;
Carry it away to mingle with the aching throb
        Of distant sorrows.

Carry it, more grave, more gentle than feeble speech,
A pitiable appeal through the ages that unroll,
To the countless hearts my fraternal love may reach,
        Appease and console.

VIRGIN

                    as a sweet apple reddens at
                    the extremity of the branch,
                    at the distant extremity:
            the fruit-pickers have forgotten
                    it or, rather, they have not
                    forgotten it, but they have
                    not been able to reach it.

As an apple, blushed and golden-skinned,
Balances itself among the verdure and sways
At the extremity of a branch where whispers and plays
            A singing, trembling wind,

As an apple against the evening sky
Laughs at the changing will of the breeze in the tree,
You shine forth, mocking the vain cupidity
            Of the covetous passerby.

The knowing ardor of autumn enfolds
In your nudity all ambers and golds.
You keep the fruit of your body beautiful
            And inaccessible.

INSCRIPTION AT THE BASE OF A STATUE

Virgins, although mute, I reply...

To those who ask, oh virgins, I intone
With tireless modulation in a voice of stone:
"Under the profound stars, my eternity
    Saddens me and crushes me.

"Serene, I see that which changes, which takes flight.
I was consecrated to Aithopia formerly,
To the ardent virgin, sister of amorous night,
    By her fond votary,

"Arista. I hear the fervency of their sighs
On summer nights whose breath grazes me like a flower
With regrets. Memorial, I immortalize
    The kisses of an hour."

*

*   *

I do not hope to touch the sky
with my two arms extended.

With two arms outstretched I do not expect
To touch the sky where mists collect;
I do not hope, as purple night nears,
    To clutch the stars.

Sapho

                    *

        *   *

              So, on the mountains, the shepherds
         trample the hyacinths underfoot, and the
              flower purples the earth.

...And wounded as a slender hyacinth,
Unhappy Atthis, you remember yet.
Your sad hair weeps, in the muffled shadow,
        Ashes of gold.

Shepherds, singing on the lonely mountain,
Fling to the evening their trembling rhythms,
And the purple flower bloodies the earth
        At the feet of passers-by.

                    *

        *   *

                   Someone, I believe, will
              remember us in the future.

On tomorrows that fate weaves from the fragile threads
   spun here
Future beings will remember what we have done;
Atthis, mistress I adore, let us not fear
        The shadow of oblivion.

For those born after us to this world where sound
The lamentations of song will cast their sighs
Toward me who loved you fiercely with an anguish profound,
        Toward you, delight of my eyes.

The fluctuating days, the perfumed nights to ensue
Will come to make eternal across the abyss
Of time the joy, the ardent suffering we knew,
        Our tremblings, our embrace, our kiss.

*

*   *

> All around, (the breeze) murmurs
> freshly through the branches of
> the apple trees, and from the
> trembling leaves runs sleep.

Coolness glides through the apple trees.
In the depth of the verdure the brook sings
The confused drone that fills a hive of bees
    With gentle murmurings.

Under the sun the summer grasses fade.
The rose, expiring after the harsh ravage
Of the heat, languishes toward the shade.
    Sleep drips from the foliage.

*

*   *

> and sleep with the blackeyes,
> (child) of the night.

The grave sunset puts out the golden light...
Appeasing all sorrows, extinguishing all joys,
Sleep, with black eyes, child of the green and quiet
  night,
    Dims the noise.

And the soul of the lilies wander in its breath, unseen,
Not knowing how to content the sighs that suspire
From the ardent sea at the foot of Mitylene,
    Tired of desire.

A VIRGIN WITH A SWEET VOICE

---a virgin with a sweet voice.

I listen, dreaming. Your refreshing voice
    Runs like the water of a spring over moss,
    Appeasing my old sorrows, my persistent loss.
In your virgin sweetness I rejoice.

                *

   *   *

Eros today has torn my soul,
wind which in the mountain
fells the oaks.

Eros has bent my soul with giant strokes
As a mountain wind twists and breaks great oaks...
And I see perish in the fire's moving light
      A whole moth flight.

*

*   *

                    ...a very delicate virgin
                            picking flowers.

I saw you plucking the fennel and the thyme
And the flower of the wind--the frail anemone--
Oh virgin. And your childlike smile I could see
      Where the dawn trembled for a time.

With the vigor of a young shrub my body came to you,
Grazed lingeringly your tender and broken flesh.
You lifted to me your eye more fresh
      Than running water or the dew.

Fatal Eros and amorous Destiny
And Aphrodite whose chosen priestess I am,
We came to cut the fennel and the thyme,
      Atthis, mistress dear to me.

*

*   *

                    I shall be always virgin.

I shall remain virgin as the serene snow
Which, in a white dream, lies there below,
Sleeping palely, that winter protects
      From the brutal sun.

As breath of the north and river of rain,
I shall flee imprint and soiling stain.
The grasp that strangles, the kiss that infects
      And wounds I shall shun.

I shall remain virgin as the distant moon
That the sobbing desires of the sea importune,
That the reaching mirror of the sea reflects,
      Never to be won.

*

*   *

The light...which does not at all
destroy the view...similar to a hyacinth.

Night, purple as a hyacinth bloom,
Your light flowers in the orchard of the skies.
Your perfume is chaste and your gentle gloom
        Consoles the eyes.

*

*   *

Predominant, as when the bard of
Lesbos dominates strangers.

Ruling the earth where resounds your lyre,
Stand up, splendid, Greek bard of Lesbos
Who alone have known the divine fire
        And laughter of Paphos.

Sappho, scatter through fathoms of space,
Disdaining the charm of the alien throngs,
The quivering of your songs which surpass
        All foreign songs.

*

*   *

...Sappho...calls Love sweet
and bitter and one who gives
sorrow...(She) names him
the weaver of chimeras.

Eros, with hands prodigal of miseries,
You spread woe, and your bitter lips have the savor
Of salt and the flowers' fragrant flavor,
        Weaver of fantasies.

THE DISDAIN OF SAPPHO

> You are nothing to me.
> As for me, I have
> no resentment whatever,
> but I have a soul serene.

You who judge me, you are nothing at all in my sight.
I have too long looked on the shadows of infinity.
I have no pride whatever in your honors, no fright
      At your calumny.

You will never know how to tarnish the devotion
Of my passion for the beauty of women, that my verse
  acclaims,
Changing as the sunsets of summer, changing as the motion
      Of waves and flames.

The dazzling foreheads that graze my life and vivify
My broken songs nothing can ever demean.
I am like a statue in the midst of passersby,
      My soul is serene.

YOU FOR WHOM I WROTE

You for whom I wrote, oh lovely young women without names,
You whom, alone, I loved, will you reread my verse
On future mornings snowing coldly on the universe,
By future quiet evenings of roses and flames?

Will you sit dreaming, amid the charming disarray
Of dishevelled hair, open robes, of her you never discover
Wherever you look: "Whether on day of mourning or festival
  day,
This woman wore always her glance, her lips of a lover."

Pale, giving forth a fragrance to haunt my flesh and mind,
In the magic evocation of the night when love should be
  rare and free
Will you say: "This woman had the ardor I can never find.
What a pity she is not living! She would have loved me!"

HOUSE OF THE PAST

II
IN THE MINOR MODE

Miraculously, here you are returned,
Seeking, along the avenue blue-burned,
    The hallowed, haunted house of the past.

Enter the dear house of tired desire at last
And see, under ceilings hollowed high like domes,
    Its people of phantoms having no homes.

Reenter the house which greets you, where I await.
Nothing has changed, though the colors are less ornate,
    The roses faded, and no dew but tears.

And here am I, the same across the years,
At the moment of return, ready to welcome you
    With the same fierce love you always knew.

HAPPY VIGIL

With love I spy upon your sleep in the night.
Your forehead has taken on the shadow's majesty,
All the enchantment, the somber mystery...
And the hour, like nocturnal water, runs in flight.

You sleep next to me, like a child. In my ear
Your breath, feeble, soft, almost musical,
Follows a steady, rhythmic rise and fall.
Your soul travels a long route, far from here.

Watching you so, I listen, love by my side.
Oh perfect visage, your tired eyes closed as in death!
Like a very distant song, your sleeping breath;
I hear it, and my heart is peaceful and satisfied.

THE SORRY HOSTELRY

The inhospitable world is like an inn
Where all is bad, where one cannot sleep for the din.

And, while the thin walls echo to the protracted screams
Of women, I seek the impossible Palace of Dreams.

I make in this hotel but a modest repast,
Longing for what could be and is not at last...

POEMS

BY

RENEE VIVIEN

TRANSLATED BY

CATHARINE KROGER

For

Bridget J. Wilson

UNDINE

Your laughter is light, your caress deep,
Your cold kisses love the harm they do;
Your eyes--blue lotus waves
And the water lilies are less pure than your face.

You flee, a fluid parting,
Your hair falls in gentle tangles;
Your voice--a treacherous tide;
Your arms--supple reeds,

Long river reeds, their embrace
Enlaces, chokes, strangles savagely,
Deep in the waves, an agony
Extinguished in a night drift.

YOUR STRANGE HAIR...

Your strange hair, cold light,
Has pale glows and blond dullness;
Your gaze has the blue of ether and waves;
Your gown has the chill of the breeze and the woods.

I burn the whiteness of your fingers with kisses.
The night air spreads the dust from many worlds.
Still I don't know anymore, in the heart of those deep
    nights,
How to see you with the passion of yesterday.

The moon grazed you with a slanted glow...
It was terrible, like prophetic lightning
Revealing the hideous below your beauty.

I saw--as one sees a flower fade--
On your mouth, like summer auroras,
The withered smile of an old whore.

53

NOCTURNE

I love your carnal lips lingering
Still creased by kisses from before.
      Your bewitching step,
And the calm perversity of your eyes
Has taken its treacherous and cold blues from the North
  sky.

Your hair, suspended like smoke,
Vaporous clear, almost immaterial,
      Seems, my love,
To receive stolen light from the darkened moon,
From a winter moon in the crystalline skies.

The voluptuous night has an alcove moistness;
The stars are like sensuous gazes
      In the gray-purple ether,
And I see spreading out, alarming and savage,
The light reflections from your cruel nails.

Underneath your gown, sliding with a bird-wing rustle,
I trace your body,--the eager lilies of your breasts,
      The pale gold under-arm,
Soft blossoming thighs, goddess legs,
The velvet belly and the curving of the loins.

The earth grows languid, weak, and the breeze,
Still warm from far away beds, comes to soften
      The ocean finally subdued...
Here is the night of love so long promised...
In the shadow I see you pale divinely.

LUCIDITY

The delicate art of vice occupies your leisure,
And you know how to awaken the hot desires
To which your wicked and supple body weakens.
The odor of the bed blends with the perfumes of your robe.
Your blond charm resembles insipid honey.
You only love the false and the artificial,
The music of words and wan murmurs.
Your kiss turns away and glides on the lips.
Your eyes are pale-starred winters.
Mournings follow your step in dreary processions.
Your gesture is a reflection, your word is a shadow.
Your body is softened under countless kisses,
And your soul is withered and your body is worn.
Languid and lewd, your sly affairs
Neglect the loyal beauty of an embrace.
You lie like one loves, and, under your fake sweetness
One senses the creeping watchful reptile.
At the foot of the shadows, like a sea without a reef,
The tombs even are less impure than your couch...
Oh Woman! I know this, but I thirst for your mouth!

MODERN-DAY NAIAD

The sea eddies luster in your robe.
Your body is the traitress tide stealing away.
You attract me like the abyss and the water;
Your supple hands have the charm of the web,
And your loose hair drifts on your breasts,
Fluid and subtle sea-weed.
This delusive attraction garnishing danger
Makes your fickle smile ever softer;
Your face recalls for me the gentle depths,
And your eyes sing to me the song of the sirens.

ON THE SAPPHIC RHYTHM

> The moon, like the Pleiades, has gone;
> it is midnight, time passes, and I
> sleep alone.
>
> —Sappho

The shadows drape themselves in widow's veils
The sea drinks the tepid blood of rivers
The fair Aphrodite, with her fickle glance,
    Laughs and dreams.

I hear moan, from the depths of space,
She who wrote the ardent and weary verses
And whose laurels flower and triumph,
    The pale Sappho.

"The nightingale gasps and trembles fitfully,
And the shadow engulfs the moon and the Pleiades:
The hour without hope and without ecstasy flees
    Into the arms of the night.

Amidst the glorious perfume of the earth,
I dream of love and I sleep alone,
Oh virgin with the beautiful face formed in ivory and gold
    Whom I weep for still!"

INVOCATION

Our eyes turned forever towards past splendors,
We evoke the fear, the pain and the torment
Of your kisses, softer than hyacinth honey,
Lover who arrogantly pours
Like one pours valerian and balm and myrrh
Before Aphrodite, Mistress of Love,
    The tempest and lightning of your lyre,
       Oh, Sappho of Lesbos!

The eager centuries lean forward to hear
The fragments of your songs. Your face is like
Winter roses found in the cinders,
And your wedding-bed ignores the sun.
Your hair falls with the ebb and flow of the sea
Like the sea algae and the somber coral
    And your desperate lips
      Drink the peace of the waters.

What does the Poet's praise matter to you,
Whose noble face is weary of eternities?
What does the echo of uneasy verses matter,
The dazzlements and the sonorities?
The music of the tides has filled your ears,
Those ocean whirlpools that murmur to her dead
    Words whose rhythm slumbers
      Like so many grave harmonies.

*

   *   *

O perfume of Paphos! Oh Poet! Oh Priestess!
Teach us the secret of divine sorrow,
Teach us longing, the relentless embrace
Where pleasure weeps, faded among the flowers!
Oh languors of Lesbos! Charm of Mytilene!
Teach us the golden verse stifled only by death,
     With your harmonious breath
         Inspire us, Sappho!

TOUCHING

The trees have kept the sun in their branches.
Veiled like a woman, evoking the past,
Dusk goes by weeping...And my fingers
Follow, quivering, the line of your thighs.

My clever fingers linger with the shudders
Of your flesh under your soft petaled gown...
The art of touching, complex and curious, equal
To the dream of perfumes, the miracle of sound.

I follow slowly the contour of your thighs,
Your shoulders, your neck, your unappeased breasts.
My delicate desire holds back from kisses:
It grazes and swoons in the white voluptuousness.

LET US GO TO MYTILENE

Softness of my songs, let us go to Mytilene
See how my soul soars once more,
Nocturnal and timid as a moth
        With golden pupils.

Let us go to the welcome of the adored virgins:
Our eyes will know the tears of returning:
We will finally see fading the places
        Of lustreless loves.

The shadow of Sappho, weaving violets
And on her face a feverish pallor,
Will smile with her silent lips
        Weary with sorrow.

There Gorgô will weep, the forsaken one,
There the eyes of Atthis will flower,
Who keeps in her flesh, wisely caressed,
        The ardor from before.

They will sing to the solemn Graces,
The golden sandals of cool mirrored Dawn,
Freshly opened roses and the eternal oceans,
        The evening star.

We will see Timas, the much grieved virgin,
Who never yielded to the torments of Eros,
And we will re-sing to an intoxicated earth
        The hymn of Lesbos.

GURINNÔ

> Mnasidika is more beautiful
> than the tender Gurinnô.

Gurinnô who weeps in the dark of my porch
Has none of your charms where Eros comes and sings,
Oh Mnasidika! Nor the splendid pride
      Of your lover's breasts.

She has none of the melted gold of your glance,
Nor the purple flower of your closed eyelids,
Nor your flesh where amber and myrrh and valerian
      Perfume the roses.

But she has known a stern voluptuousness,
The fear of love and the shadows coming on...
One night I drank unwillingly
      From her bitter lips.

ALL IS WHITE

> The stars around the beautiful
> moon veil their clear faces as
> soon as, in her plenty, she
> illumines the earth with silver
> glows.

All is white, the moon offers her abundance,
At her feet whines the tormented ocean:
Serene, she sees the flowering of solitude
      And chastity.

The stars, before the divine Selene,
Have veiled their faces, and the clearness, snowing
From the virgin clear sky, illumines
      The silver earth.

I WILL STAY VIRGIN

I will always remain virgin.

I will stay virgin like snow
Serene, sleeping white,
Sleeping pale, that the winter protects
  From the brutal sun.

Like the river water and the North Wind
I will not know stains and foot prints.
I will escape the horrible embrace,
  And the corroding kiss.

I will stay virgin like the moon
Reflected in the glass tide,
Troubled by the long sigh of desire
  For the ocean.

SIMILAR LIPS

The odor of the freesia flees
Towards the black murmuring cypress...
The loving dusk and the night
Have merged their hair.

I saw them mingle, when the nightshade
Gleamed, bathed in moonlight,
The somber hair of the night
With the pale hair of the dusk.

The balsamic day's ending,
Flaxen with drones and bees,
Senses, with a love kiss,
The beauty of similar lips.

The odor of the freesia flees
Towards the black murmuring cypress...
The loving dusk and the night
Have merged their hair.

WHITEHAIRED WOMEN

> You who talk little, white-
> haired women, you, flowers
> of old age on earth.

Whitehaired women, winter caressed,
You who rejoice in the intimacy of the fire
And of the dusk, oh flowers of old age,
     You who speak little,

You have the candid peace of many years,
You are the chorus of living memories:
Soft, you twine the faded garlands
     Of old dreams.

You linger, as before, on porches
Where Phoebus bleached the moss and the lichen,
And smiling you light the red torches
     Of hymens.

You love the brown-eyed autumn and the clatter
Of doors where the wind leaves a salty taste:
You spin, by the song of your humble wheel,
     The snowy flax.

The virgin respects and fears your wisdom,
And your greetings are slow like a good-bye,
Whitehaired women, flowers of old age,
     You who speak little....

LOVE POEM

                    Oh you, who flirt through the
                    windows, virgin in your head,
                    woman below.

Oh you, you who knew how to flirt,
Blue like the midnights, through the windows,
I saw you on the road where I wandered here or there
Through the odors, hours and the meadow laughter.

The sun bleached your hair with one long ray,
Your eyes stabbed me with a double flame;
I saw you, lovely woman! and mused on
Your virgin face and your womanly thighs.

I saw you on the road where I wandered here or there
Through the shadows, hours and the meadow laughter,
Oh you, who knew how to flirt,
Blue like the midnights, through the windows.

ON THE IMAGE OF SABAITHIS

You can recognize her even from
here. See: with Sabaithis,
it's her physical image and a
generous soul. See her serenity;
I think I can also see her
softness. Be joyful, happy woman.

Those who have never seen her admire Sabaithis.
Far off, one contemplates her in her present beauty:
Her rose arms and her azure eyes
And her golden hair that the breeze torments.

Passing, pause in front of her fresh gaze
Animated by the flame of clear wisdom,
And in these traits, softer than honey and valerian
Recognize the visible splendor of her soul.

Keep the tender peace on your face, and smile
In your double splendor of virgin and lover,
Immortal in the midst of barren rosebushes...
A salute to your triumph, blessed woman!

WORDS TO A LOVER

Understand me: I am a mediocre being,
Neither good nor very bad, quiet, a bit sullen.
I hate heavy perfumes and loud voices,
And grey is more dear to me than scarlet or ochre.

I love sunset, the day dying bit by bit,
The fire, the monastic intimacy of a room
Where the lamps with veiled amber transparence
Redden the old bronze and blue the stoneware.

My eyes on the carpet, more polished than sand,
I idly recreate the golden river-banks
Where the clarity of beautiful yesterdays still linger...
And yet I am so much to blame.

See: I am at the age where a woman abandons herself
To a man whom her weakness searched out but whom she
    dreads,
And I have never given myself like that
Because you appeared from around the corner.

The hyacinth bleeds the hillsides red,
You dreamt and love walked beside you...
I am a woman, I have no right to your beauty.
I have been condemned to masculine ugliness.

And I would have the inexcusable audacity to desire
Your gentle and sisterly love,
The light step which does not crush the ferns
And the soft voice that has just gone into the night.

I have been forbidden your hair, your eyes,
Because your hair is long and full of scent
And because your eyes have strange desires
Like rebellious waves.

I have been told off with irritated gestures,
Because my gaze searched for your tender response...
Watching us pass, no one wanted to understand
That I chose you simply.

Consider the worthless law I break
And judge my love, which knows no wrong,
As candid, as necessary and as fatal
As the desire that joins lover and mistress.

*

No one read the light in my eyes
On the road where my lover led me,
And they said: "Who is that cursed woman
Who deafly courts the flames of hell?"

Let us leave them to the cares of their impure morality,
And let us dream that dawn is honey flaxen,
That day comes unsoured and night without malice
Like friends whose goodness reassures us........

We will see the star-light on mountains....
What does the judgment of men matter to us?
And what must we fear, for we are
Pure facing life and we love each other?.....

A L'Heure des mains jointes

LET A WAVE TAKE IT...

The tide, asleep, breathes evenly,
The soul of the conch shells floats and makes noise on the
    shore...
All is hostile to me, and my youth aches.
I am tired of loving fugitive forms.
Standing tall, I take my heart where yesterday love was
So vibrant, and here: I throw it into the ocean.

Let a light dancing wave take it,
Let the ocean merge it into her deep work
And take it where she pleases, like a dead thing,
Let an eddy suspend it in the coral branches,
Let the will of the colliding winds lift it
And let it roll amongst the shingle, on the shore.

Let it waver and float, one night, imprisoned
By the long hair of the blond seaweed,
Let the wishes of the calm waters be given to her
In the false twilight of the waves...
And let my heart, finally subdued,
Tranquil and soft, obey the will of the wind and of the
    eddies.

I throw it into the ocean, like the ring of the Doges,
The golden ring that careless tides have tarnished
And which falls, amidst the song and the praise,
Into the transparent blue, into the infinite green...
Time is vast, the delightful dead are in it,
And I give my heart to the eternal ocean.

I LOVE YOU FOR BEING...

I love you for being weak and caressing in my arms
And for searching the certain shelter of my arms
Like a warm cradle where you will rest.

I love you for being a redhead and like autumn,
Frail image of the Goddess of autumn
That the setting sun lights and crowns.

I love you for being slow and for walking without noise
And for talking very low and for hating noise,
Like one does in the presence of night.

And I love you above all for being pale and dying,
And for moaning with the tears of dying
In the cruel pleasure that tears and torments.

I love you for being, sister of queens of old,
Exiled in the midst of splendors of old,
Whiter than the moon's reflection on a lily.

I love you for never being moved, when, pale
And trembling, I can't hide my face, pale,
Oh you, who will never know how much I love you.

YOU FOR WHOM I WROTE

You for whom I wrote, oh beautiful young women!
You whom alone I loved, will you reread my poems
In the future mornings snowing onto the universe
And in the future evenings of roses and flames?

Will you dream, amongst the charming disorder
Of your scattered hair, and your undone robes:
"This woman, through tears and joy
Maintained her gaze and her lover's lips."

Pale and breathing your embalmed flesh
In the magic evocation of the night,
Will you say: "This woman had the passion that escapes
   me...
How alive she is! She would have loved me...."

IN THE FUTURE EVENINGS

No! in the future evenings of roses and flames,
As mysterious as hindu temples,
No one will know my name and no one amongst you
Will repeat my poems, oh beautiful young women!

No one amongst you will have the charming whim,
While suffering over an impossible woman,
To call very low, pale and desiring,
For my domineering lover's lips.

You will search for love, fresh and perfumed,
Turning your resolute steps towards the future,
And no one amongst you will remember
Me, who has loved you so deeply.

UNION

Our heart is the same in our woman's breast,
My dearest! Our body is made the same.
A similar heavy destiny has weighted our soul,
We love each other and we are the perfect hymn.

I decipher your smile and the shadow on your face.
My softness is the same as your great softness,
Sometimes it even seems that we are of the same race...
I love in you my child, my friend and my sister.

Like you I love the lonely water, the breeze,
The far-away, the stillness and the handsome violet...
With the power of my love, I understood you:
I know exactly what pleases you.

See, I am more than yours, I am you.
You have no cares that aren't mine also...
And what could you love that I don't also?
And what could you think that I don't also?

Our love is part of infinity,
Absolute as death and beauty...
See, our hearts are joined and our hands are united
Firmly in space and in eternity.

SAD WORDS

What sadness now, after our pleasure, dearest,
Our last kiss, like a sob,
Falls from your pale mouth
And sad and slow, no words,
You walk away, heavy, Oh my love!

The sadness of our weary love-making, nights,
Comes like the pain of parting
Comes like the poems that don't move us anymore
Passes like the black imperial march,
The dark sound of torches towards evening...

And I know you feel cheated and I feel distant...
We stay together, with the eyes of exile,
And a thin, gold string holds us,
With weary eyes, we follow our flown dream...
Gone already, you smile, far away.

ROSES RISING

My brunette with the golden eyes, your ivory body, your
    amber
Has left bright reflections in the room
        Above the garden.

The clear midnight sky, under my closed lids,
Still shines...I am drunk from so many roses
        Redder than wine.

Leaving their garden, the roses have followed me...
I drink their brief breath, I breathe their life.
        All of them are here.

It's a miracle...The stars have risen,
Hastily, across the wide windows
        Where the melted gold pours.

Now, among the roses and the stars,
You, here in my room, loosening your robe,
        And your nakedness glistens.

Your unspeakable gaze rests on my eyes...
Without stars and without flowers, I dream the impossible
        In the cold night.

MARY'S SEVEN LILIES

The seven lilies flowered in front of the ancient porch.
Each one of them longer and straighter than a torch,
Their pistils are like the flames of a torch.

The seven lilies flowered miraculously
In the august silence and in the shadow, the moment
Christ rose, miraculously...

Under the saintly hands of the priest
In the shadow and in the incense, one saw them appear...
Then the people saw him smile, the old priest...

And everyone watched them with eyes of love.
The priest, looking all around, said:
"My brothers, behold the flowers of Saintly-Love!"

Their perfume rose towards the divine vision.
Everyone understood the meaning of the glorious message
On the altar where Mary hears the Message.

And the lilies poured out peace around themselves
And the host shone duller than they,
The transparent Host was less white than they...

Appear again, Oh seven lilies of Mary,
When the crowd on its knees cries and prays!
Appear again in honor of Mary!

BIRDS IN THE NIGHT

Last night, birds sang in my heart...
A good ending for all my past bitterness...
I heard those birds singing in my heart.

In my heartbreak, night was merciful
And as tender as a lover could be.
It's a rare night that shows itself merciful.

In its shadow, I heard the bird song
And finally slept...My dreams were beautiful
For having heard the bird song....

PILGRIMAGE

It seems as if I have neither sex nor age,
My troubles have so abruptly overcome me.
Time has woven itself...And here I am barefooted,
Finishing the terrible and long pilgrimage...

I know that the golden dawn knows only how to deceive,
That youth is wrong to follow shadows,
That eyes betrayed...My lips are bitter...
Ah! How long the road is and how far away the evening!

And the procession, slow and sad, continues
With the supplicants who weary of the road.
Sometimes someone lifts me up, a woman reaches her hand,
And all of us beseech the tranquil Divine Night.

EPITAPH ON A TOMB STONE

Here the door from which I leave...
Oh my roses and my thorns!
Never mind the past. I sleep
Dreaming about divine things...

Here then is my ravished soul
Because she is calm and asleep
Having, for the love of Death,
Pardoned the crime: Life.

*

*   *

*

THE TRANSLATORS

*****

JEANNETTE H. FOSTER.

Dr. Foster is well-known for her classic SEX VARIANT
WOMEN IN LITERATURE (New York: Vantage Press, 1956;
Baltimore: Diana Press, 1976). Her interest in Renée
Vivien has already been demonstrated by her
translation of the poet's only novel, A WOMAN
APPEARED TO ME, published in 1976 by THE NAIAD PRESS.

MARGARET PORTER.

Under the pseudonym of Gabrielle l'Autre, Margaret A.
Porter published her translations of some of Renée
Vivien's poems in THE LADDER, the magazine which was
for sixteen years the principal voice of the Lesbian
community. A poet in her own right, her work has
appeared in many books and magazines.

CATHARINE KROGER.

Catharine Elisabeth Kroger is a young poet who, in
1976, obtained her Master of Arts degree from the San
Diego State University with a thesis on Renée Vivien
and her poetry. This is her first appearance as a
translator for publication.

BIBLIOGRAPHICAL NOTE

The POEMES de RENÉE VIVIEN were published in a
two-volume set by Alphonse Lemerre, Paris,
1923-24.

CONTENTS: Vol. I   Études et préludes
                       Cendres et poussières
                       Évocations
                       Sapho
                       La Vénus des aveugles

             Vol. II   Les Kitharèdes
                       A L'Heure des mains jointes
                       Sillages
                       Flambeaux éteints
                       Dans un coin de violettes
                       La Vent des vaisseaux
                       Haillons

This two-volume edition has been reprinted in
facsimile by the Arno Press, Inc., 1975, in
one volume.

The poems presented in translation here have
been identified by the title of the collection
in which they appear in the French.

Other Publications of THE NAIAD PRESS

THE LATECOMER, by Sarah Aldridge. A Novel. 107 pages.
ISBN 0-930044-00-2 $3.00

TOTTIE, by Sarah Aldridge. A Novel. 181 pages.
ISBN 0-930044-01-0 $4.50

CYTHEREA'S BREATH, by Sarah Aldridge. A Novel. 240 pages.
ISBN 0-930044-02-9 $5.00

SPEAK OUT, MY HEART, by Robin Jordan. A Novel. 148 pages.
ISBN 0-930044-03-7 $4.00

A WOMAN APPEARED TO ME, by Renée Vivien, Translated from
the French by Jeannette H. Foster. A Novel, with
Introduction by Gayle Rubin. xli, 90 pages.
ISBN 0-930044-06-1 $4.00

LESBIANA, by Barbara Grier. Book reviews from THE LADDER.
iv, 309 pages.
ISBN 0-930044-05-3 $5.00

LOVE IMAGE, by Valerie Taylor. A Novel. 168 pages.
ISBN 0-930044-08-8 $4.50

Also obtainable from THE NAIAD PRESS:

THE LESBIAN IN LITERATURE, A Bibliography,
Compiled by Gene Damon, Jan Watson,
and Robin Jordan. 96 pages. $7.00

THE NAIAD PRESS, INC.
20 Rue Jacob Acres
Bates City, Missouri 64011

Mail Orders Welcome

Please Include 10% Postage